THE DEPTH OF WELLS

Maren C. Tirabassi

Peter E. Randall Publisher
Portsmouth, New Hampshire
2000

ACKNOWLEDGEMENTS

Grateful acknowledgement is made to these magazines and newspapers in which some poems appeared previously, sometimes in slightly different form: *The Other Side, Re-Imagining: Quarterly Publication of the Re-Imagining Community, Open Hands: Resources for Ministries Affirming the Diversity of Human Sexuality, Compass Rose: The White Pines College Journal of Art and Writing, The Granite Review, Kettle of Fish, Garden Lane, Victory Park: The Journal of the New Hampshire Institute of Art, Lawrence (Ma.) Eagle Tribune, Waterville (Me.) Morning Sentinel.*

"The 761st Meeting of the Esther Beecher Guild" appears in the book *Finding Time, Finding Energy – The Future of Women's Church Groups* by Allison Stokes, (Ash Grove Press, 1996).

Cover art and design by Diane St. Jean

Peter E. Randall Publisher
    Box 4726, Portsmouth, NH 03802

Distributed by
    University Press of New England
    Hanover and London

Library of Congress Cataloging in Publication Data
Tirabassi, Maren C.
    The depth of wells/ Maren C. Tirabassi
        p.cm.
    ISBN 0-914339-82-6
    1. Christian poetry, American. I. Title
PS3570.I68 D46 1999
811'.54--dc21
                                                    99-052532

For pastoring me over these years of my pastoring,
I dedicate this book to

Charles H. Harper,
who walked with me across the longest bridge,

and Carole C. Carlson,
who taught me that one rain can change everything.

CONTENTS

PREACHER AND POET

Preacher tells a text
and, from the
heart of a word
spoken long ago
in good news,
reclaims the
new birth,
or lets
the buried life
fly free
to heal and hope
a world grown sad.

Poet looks within
tender images
clinging to self
and scalpels off
a wonder known
under the edge
of knowing,
or a phrase
of the story
that intimate
and universal
is life.

It hurts more,
to be a poet
than a preacher.
It hurts most,
like raw miracle
or unexpected
healing,
to carry
both voices
and still hear
what it is
to be lonely.

INTRODUCTION

For twenty years I have climbed into pulpits and looked around at the gentle, lonely, happy, doubting faces of people sitting in the long wooden pews of New England churches. These have been city sanctuaries, suburb sanctuaries and country sanctuaries – and the faces have been different . . . and the same. Some of these people I have come to know more intimately because I've visited them in hospitals, coaxed them through Christmas pageants, been privileged to murmur around their loves and losses the old familiar words of wedding and funeral.

For the last seven years, I've also been fortunate enough to teach the writing of poetry in churches, schools and prisons, and the people I've met in class, writing with pencils and hearts, are also reflected in these pages.

Many of the poems in *The Depth of Wells* are stories which I have drawn out of the experiences of folks I've known. These are not "factual" stories because the facts and details of several different lives are splashed together in the bucket of my imagination. Nevertheless, they are certainly "true" stories, if truth is, after all, something about ground water and source. I am very grateful to the many people whose stories I have drawn upon so deeply.

[handwritten margin note: what a good way to put it]

My own story as pastor and poet flows through the book and for time, support, advice and affirmation I thank my husband Donald, my children Matthew and Maria, and my parents Russell and Elizabeth Snider. In the mutual critique of three Seacoast New Hampshire poetry groups these poems have been shaped – Pat Parnell alone has trimmed many an over-extended image. For reading and helping to select this collection, thanks to Joan Jordan Grant, Les Norman, Mark Burrows, Diane Karr, and Kim Sadler. For the wonderful design of the cover which reminds me of living water, I thank Diane St. Jean, and for gracefully producing this volume, I thank Peter Randall.

ADVENT — A PROLOGUE

I Walk the Shore in Advent

I walk the shore in Advent –
salt water ice
mixes with sand
and it is the only time of year
when I look back the way I've come
to see no footprints
and I must trust my memory
that I have come from anywhere.

But I walk the empty mile of beach
to feel the chosen absence of the season.
There is an ebbtide of waiting,
watching the shadow
where God will be.

The ocean surges and pulls
a moving threshold
of holiness,
and all along the horizon
rhythms the pulse of incarnation
by breaker and undertow,
and I can hear in the cold wind
tasting of the promise of snow
a wild and lonely
carol of the waves.

CEREMONY

They came Thursday at noon –
saying they heard that the lady
of the house married people.
Paul is sandy-haired
with grey in his beard.
He makes his living
with horses and carriages.
He wore a leather jacket,
wide-brimmed brown
felt hat and jeans.
Gay is short and runs her fingers
through tousled blond hair.
There's laughter like country music
under her voice all the time.
She wore a tight purple skirt,
tall black boots,
and tinsel earrings.

They said they met a month ago
and are so much in love
they think they
think each other's thoughts.
They are building
a log house in Colebrook.
Paul and Gay didn't exactly
tell their children
they were eloping today.

For me, too, it was love at first sight –
the real wedding of it all,
not interrupted by plans.
Of course, I didn't have my
congregational manual,
or my black robe,
or an aisle or an organ,
but I pinned a silver cross
with a purple stone in it

on my dress,
and opened a poetry book
where I remembered
there is a simple service.

I lit the Christmas tree lights
against the solstice gloom
and the air was soft
with candle scent and pine.
They stood there
by mother's rocker
on the old blue rag rug.
The brown and white terrier
curled up at their feet,
content to be the witness,
and we repeated
gentle old-fashioned
promises,
and they exchanged
very bright new gold rings,

and Gay cried.

Then I said a prayer for them
and I know they were surprised
and pleased, and
so was God,
and they drove north in the
cold December rain
to honeymoon
somewhere in Maine –
they didn't know where –
but they would know
when it was right
to stop and
begin to be married,
reverently and not lightly.

COMMUNION

One of those long church days
sometime between the late afternoon
nursing home visit and the
evening deacons' meeting,
eating bag-supper alone at my desk,
no lamps lit against December sunset –
Connie phoned,
voice sharp in the darkness.
Bob was not home and she could not lift
Cathy from the dinner table
and get her ready for bed

and would I come?

I stood in front of the young woman,
hands under shoulders hollow as bird wing,
and, with her mother behind,
Cathy shifted her frail weight forward,
balanced to the bathroom
and sank into the hospital bed
someone had carried
over those narrow stairs.

There was a wild-woman striped hat
on the bed frame.
the breast cancer support group
bought for each other
the most outlandish hats,
and then died, one by one,
in Boston hospitals –
died in their passionate hats.

Cathy understands the cancer.
She is a pharmacist.
She loves lilac-time and Christmas Eve,
and birthdays – especially
her daughter Carrie's

eight-year-old birthday.
Cathy used to make quilts and candles.
She traveled and had many friends.
She used to live
on Martha's Vineyard.

Now, in this Cape Ann winter twilight,
awkwardly supported
by her own mother and a minister
she met only a couple months ago,
she knew better than we
that she couldn't stand up,
even for Carrie,
against death much longer.

For Cathy now – it has come to
accepting help,
giving simple thanks for breath itself,
trying to smile and rest and
compose her face
for us
in lines of peace,
just one more Christmas –
for she will not see lilacs
or any new birthdays.

And as for me – back in the church
I took my bag-supper
into the night-time sanctuary,
put the sandwich on the
communion table,
muttered a few words they teach
pastors to say,
and stood there in the dark

to cry on the bread.

Christmas Eve
at the Epsom Circle McDonald's

The kids with the santa hats
are selling hamburgers
more cheerfully
because they feel the season
and are glad for early closing.
A boyfriend comes in
and hangs over the counter
pressing against
tattered garland
looped to the finger level
of children.

A family with three toddlers,
jazzy with excitement,
are traveling to Maine
in the drizzle
of the holy evening.
The littlest boy
in red and green plaid
oshkosh runs in circles,
strangling french fries
in his hand.
Tired of the car and
already eager for
presents and bed,
his little sneakers tramp
like angel feet.

An older couple
in a corner talk quietly
about their daughter
who's been dead
four christmases now.
They could have gone
to their son-in-law's house.

His kind new wife
invited them with her family,
but it didn't seem right.
And this was the very
brightest place – it
looked like a star
when they drove down
the highway, and
they knew there would be
children here.

A divorced Dad with
Budweiser on a black T-shirt
jokes with his
six year old daughter
over milk shakes.
A clumsily wrapped present
perches on the
molded plastic seat.
He is trying to make
the very best treat he can
of their christmas hour
before bringing her
back to her Mom's house.
Brown eyes shine at him
and he thinks
she is excited for later –
for Santa and all –
but she's looking at him
all over
memorizing the gift.

The preacher
is on her way to church
to remember Bethlehem
out loud
for the folks who come
to break bread and
light little candles
with paper circles on them

that keep the wax
from dripping on their hands
as they sing "silent night."
Most of them
have heard the story
about the child before,
and so has she.
She has come here first,
just to sit for a while
and watch the
christmas eve communion.

WINTER

WALKING IN MAINE

I walk along the narrows
over grey rock,
crunching the shell shatters
of old gulls' feast.
The grey-white tree bones
bend in wind
that cuts my face
and draws tears.

I have come to Maine
to cry.

Green of conifer,
sleeps in the quiet hills,
beyond the bay, distance
softening horizon.

The broken shell of whelk
or moon snail
lie in my hands –
the spiral is exposed.

My life is turning
and chambered,
secret, sometimes even
without prayer, so
holy is the twist
of hidden music
of the sea.

THE FRIENDMAKER

The old woman was a friendmaker all her life –
not the kind who clings
to family or the acquaintances of childhood
or college friends,
but who cares herself
into all the people around her
as they change with the shifting seasons of life.
In fact, it was often the young ones
who sat at the well of her listening -
the teenager hugging some failure,
the lonely latchkey child,
she could teach rummy,
or the couple in love
across racial barriers or class,
or perhaps gay or lesbian partners
needing a plate
of Christmas cookies.

When the limits of her body drew in
and she went to live in a nursing home,
her room was the refuge
where aides would bring a cup of coffee,
and the housekeeping staff would rest on their mops
for a few minutes
because she remembered
their children's names,
even the complicated foreign ones.

And so, of course, after the stroke,
when she couldn't move much, or talk at all,
she made a new friend of the tree
outside her window,
with no regrets.
She carefully watched its spring gifts
of blossom and leaf,
the July sun and shadow
mingle in its branches

playing stories across the stucco wall,
the wind harp it an autumn sonata
with much rattling
dry-leaf percussion.

And in the winter time one cold year
at three-thirty in the morning
the friendmaker woke up to discover
in the bare beauty
of the tree's skeleton
under the full moon of January –
a secret silhouette of its soul.

CHRISTENING

I baptize Meredith, two years old.
It is after worship
because she had a full-scale
"no-water" tantrum
in the middle of the service,
and her parents took her downstairs.

The last of the choir members
disrobes and walks away
with a dry rustle of sheet music.
Thin pungent smoke rises
from newly extinguished candles
and the pews settle with wooden sighs
for the week's rest.

We sit on thick red sanctuary carpet
with a bowl of water between us
and Meredith splashes
with great pleasure
and makes the water dance.
She has watched
what happens to other children.
She places her hand solemnly and softly
on her mother's head
three times, murmuring
something secret and sacred,
and then blesses her father's hair,
and strokes mine.

Only then am I given the bowl
with great dignity,
and my fingers touch her,
explore the fragile childhood bones
of her temple,
wet her forehead and curls,
and whisper - holy, holy, holy.

A SMALL REMEMBERING

Cry for the sisters of the broken bread.
Cry for the beaten prayers,
the vulnerable chapel,
the humble laughter
of women growing older.
Cry for the sabbath evening,
with candles of welcome,
wick-dimmed by tears.
Cry for the home of women where
still there are women who sing.

Pray for the sisters of the broken bread.
Pray for Edna Mary
and for Marie Julien.
gathered now in angel-wing,
comforted by quiet waters.
Pray for those who were deeply
wounded, for Mary Anna
and Patricia, pray that
as bruises darken and fade
their terror slowly heals.

Of blessed sacrament you were the
servant-sisters, and, now,
you who kept vigil
have become the host.
Your cries and your prayers
are consecrated.
Your battered hospitality is holy,
and your pain and your death
are as sacred as the old pain
and the old spreadeagled
death of God.

Lift up your hearts.

We lift them up, and lift up
our broken bread –
in remembrance of you.

[This poem is written for the women who were attacked at the Convent of the Servants of the Blessed Sacrament in Waterville, Maine, in January, 1996, and for all clergywomen and women religious who feel the chill of fear within their commitment to hospitality and yet do not bar their doors.]

LANGDON

the spare Yankee
with the long thin face
like cool sculpture under skin,
and the large quiet hands
folded his tall frame
into the pastor's study chair.

A deacon in his day,
he taught the eighth grade boys
so long they named
the room for him.
He still cooks the homeless meal
once a month,
makes the men take off their hats
before he says grace.
He loved his wife,
worked hard all his life in
the foundry at United Shoe. Honest,
uncomfortably honest,
he probed four or five ministers
over eighty years
with questions.
Langdon never let a convenient
hypocrisy pass, or any
cheap theology.

I thought it was my turn.
No, he said he'd never wanted to ask
these things of anyone before,

maybe he was getting older.

He wanted to know
what kind of cruel God it could mean,
if Jesus died for our sins?
And what about red letter Bibles?
How could anyone know

what was said in Gethsemane?
And isn't the resurrection
just a myth?
Didn't I really think
what we have here is all there is?

So straightbacked and sad
he sat there
with his honorable doubts
fine like tested steel.

And I wanted to take
those long bony fingers
into my small hands and pray,
but instead I offered
him a respect that was far
more intimate.

I didn't give him an answer
that I don't have.

ON GOING TO A FORMAL PARTY

Eyeshadow – green, vivid,
(I look like a hooker),
nailpolish too gummy –
kitchen fluff stuck
to the thumbs.
The score is three
runs for the stockings,
before I squirm into home.

(I become intensely
aware of the delicacy
of the fabric of life.)

My scuffed shoes look
all their age and
half their price tonight –
so do I.
My dress hem is uneven
and screams the bargain
which pleased me before,
like some flamboyant
orange bird – "Cheap, cheap".

I am fatter than yesterday;
my hair has grown
too long;
I have cramps; and
I will absolutely,
abysmally, humiliatingly,
without question, mercy,
or cavil,
have
nothing ... nothing ...
nothing ...
to say.

THE MIRACLE

The hospice nurse said
that when the young man died
they had classical music
on the radio –
Bach, she thought,
but wasn't sure,
because she was busy,
and just glad that everyone
arrived in time to say "good-bye"
and that the pain medicine
was strong enough, and the
bubbling red froth
from his lungs
was less noisy
than it had been for days.

She was proud of them –
the young man's sister
and brother-in-law –
keeping him home
when no one thought
they could, or should even try.
They put the hospital bed
in the corner of the dining room
so he could watch
nieces and a nephew
doing math and English homework
at the big oak table
almost every night.

He sat in the midst of their
Thanksgiving dinner
with its turkey and pie scents,
the visitor-laughter, and
even the football later,
because they brought the
television right into the room.

It was awkward
when Dan coughed a lot,
but the men covered it
with loud advice
to the quarterback
and touch down cheers.

It was closer to the end
when the carolers from the church
came to sing hearty off-key
hark-the-heralds
for cocoa,
and when they started
"Silent Night", it became
softer and softer
because the adults dropped out
one by one
with tears in their throats,
until the little children
were left to sing
the last verse alone.

But all that's beside the point.

The story that
the hospice nurse
wanted to share with everyone
was that the moment Dan died
the Bach, or whatever it was,
faded out,
and somebody at the
radio station
must have played "He's Got
the Whole World in His Hands"–
though it was only
a line or two
of the spiritual that they heard –
and she wanted
everyone to know
she had been present
for a miracle.

SERENITY

"The most significant thing
about my adolescence
happened
to someone else,"
the young woman said
from one of the back rows
of the A.A. meeting.

"My Dad quit
when I was thirteen,
and I was supposed to be happy,
even if it was too late
for me to have
my childhood back.

But it was too big.

It took all the air away –
just when I was going to have a life,
nothing left for me,
but to repeat his
atonement."

SYLVIA IN THE WRITING CLASS

Sylvia sleeps in her living room, she says,
by the pretty lights of the
Christmas tree,
and she is not so lonely
under gold and green and the reflection
of silver tinsel on red balls.

Sylvia writes stories of her childhood –
dear doctor father, gentle mother,
upright Boston philanthropic
grandmama . . .
and the Christmas she had smallpox
after dancing till midnight with
the handsome Philadelphia boys
in her neat blue satin shoes . . .
and the time she stood
in Convention Hall when they
nominated Roosevelt
for a second term and, how,
lifted by the roar of the applause,
she squeezed her brother's hand,
so proud to be a Democrat ...

Sylvia writes stories of her childhood,
and also stories about the children
next door,
so much younger than her own sons,

then she is not so lonely.

Sylvia sleeps in her living room
by the pretty lights of the
Christmas tree,

while the days of January
slip away...
and March and April.

THE 761ST MEETING
OF THE ESTHER BEECHER GUILD

The old women around the table
in the glow of the lamp
are telling stories.
The snow is heaped high outside
and they have no desire to go
back to where each lives alone.
They have already talked of
death, nursing homes,
and friends,
and they are feeling
fortunate.
          Josephine
Burnham, Lois Rodgers,
Olivia Standish,
Maureen Allen and Eunice Pride.

Maureen remembers coming to America
as a girl – two girls from Ireland
in steerage – with money
wrapped in cloth bags on
strings around their necks,
sleepless and excited
the night before landing,
desperate to hide
their ignorance –
what is a statue of liberty?

Livy of late finds it easier to focus
on long ago than yesterday,
so her stories are about
growing up in Lee,
New Hampshire.
The snow now reminds her
of church-going
with her family in the sleigh,

and, that, when she was
very good,
she could hang on behind
riding skis.

Jo ("why are kids so different these days?!")
Burnham recounts her
high school trip,
taking the boat to New York,
the train to Philadelphia
and Washington.
She cannot now recall any of
the very famous places
they must have visited,
but, oh, how they
danced on the boat.

And then all five begin to talk,
for some reason, of wells –
Lo and Eunice have them still,
but all remember
pumps in the kitchen sink,
and how those deacons
fought to keep outhouses
at the church,
even after plumbing
finally came to Cape Ann.

And there it ends –
Not much.

As outside the window an
afternoon sun licks
plow-sculpted snow
pink and peach and golden,
inside, inside a circle of
lamplight,
old women talk
about the depth of wells.

SPRING

Vernal Equinox

The forsythia is beginning to bloom
and it looks like a young girl.

People are test-riding bikes
at Bicycle Bob's,
and laying mean-tire rubber spin marks
around the parking lot,
dreaming of freedom and road.

The groom with Merlin-old eyebrows
under the wedding oak
has begun to dance
with his beautiful bride, Lucy.
She has star-like white flowers in her hair
and one of the silver straps
of her borrowed dress
has fallen off a vulnerable shoulder.
Their grown children
from other marriages laugh
with joy that comes up
somewhere deep from the music
or the night or the love.

In another part of the city
homeless people
are lining up for wooden quart boxes
of bright-juicy strawberries,
confiscated from some vendor
who didn't have a license,
and they are biting the extravagant red fruit
(after the usual day-old bread,
thin soup and sweet coffee)
like people come to Eucharist –
some quick and furtive
and some with wild abandon,
all tongues and lip.

It is spring, and the poet
cannot decide which poem to hunt further
into the wide open mouth
of early evening words.

CONFESSION

The old woman sits
by the kitchen table.
We have pushed coffee cups
into the center of
the yellow oilskin cloth,
and I am absentmindedly
brushing cookie crumbs
into a small pile.

She starts to speak
and then hesitates,
and so I look into
her faded blue eyes
surrounded by
soft-worn wrinkles
and try to nudge her
with my silence.

"You see, my husband
shot me one night –
right in the leg.
Said he was going
to get that raccoon, and
I was out by the woodpile
bringing in washing
just before dark.
Bullet went clean out
the other side of the shed
and we never had to
call any doctor."

It is really spring today
and crocus is breaking soil,
like bones rising.
She folds an inch
of her apron seam
between thumb and first finger
again and again,

and looks – not now
at my face, but
at the white curtain,
blowing in the gentle air
that comes fresh through
the open window.

"I promised I would never tell."

REQUIEM

Day after day he works
to clear out the old cemetery
behind our house.
Jim knocked at the door
that first day to tell me
that he just moved back
to Portsmouth,
and he means to tend
the old family plot,
tear out the thorn bushes
and poison ivy,
paint black again the rusty fence,
plant grass and flowers.

His mother, Muriel, was buried here
only twenty years ago –
but before her,
it was nearly ninety years
since a grave was opened,
and the names buried are all
last century names –
Lemuel and Beulah his wife,
Rufus and John,
Lydia, Ruth, Lemuel again,
then three together –
Etty and Jessie and Sadie,
the oldest only four.

He asked about the single stone
broken and lying outside
the railing, almost lost
in weeds and leaves,
and, for some reason
I don't tell him the story
the house agent told me
when we moved in here –
that Olivia had a child

out of wedlock
and they wouldn't let her rest
next to the tall monument for the
gallant only son, or more
modest markers for
the Civil War lieutenant,
the spinster sister,
and the little girls.

Unforgiven when she was alive,
and unforgiven still.

Jim's done now for the day –
I watch him walk away in sunset,
and I envy him a little
his reclaiming the old graveyard.
I have jobs like that
in my life, but they are
always more metaphor
than undergrowth,
and I can't always rake up
the brush of them.

I need to let him do undeterred
what he has come to do,
perhaps some remembering
of his mother, or
some digging down thing
in his own life,
but I know that sometime
before he is finished
I will tell him about Olivia,
because if he is
going to make it holy again
above the old skulls and femurs,
he'll have to know
what is really buried here

and what he might disturb.

Be All You Can Be

She was a beauty pageant queen,
Miss Teen Vermont,
and, when she went into the Army,
she bought a scrapbook
with a blue cover
to paste in
newspaper clippings
of high school triumphs –
local store openings and
Old Home Day parades.

In the Virginia barracks
the women bunked downstairs
with no doors.
She was sleeping on her stomach
when her face was pushed
into the pillow
and she was raped
from behind.
She didn't say anything.
The girl who slept there before
was put in the mental
health block,
and nobody saw her again.

In Germany, her sergeant raped her,
and then he phoned
her mom and dad
to fly overseas and get her
from the Berlin hospital
after her failure at suicide.
The military discharged her –
with an honorable discharge,
marked "personality disorder".
Personality disorder
means there won't be
a discharge hearing,

and later they lost her
medical records.

But after all, she had already
torn up her scrapbook.

Spring Poem for Amy Marie

The old woman in her letter
asked for a poem about spring.
She mentioned forsythia
cut in her room
in the Canterbury nursing home.
She had been an arranger of flowers
years ago –
a pastor's wife,
putting pussy willows on the altar.
Now, a college girl volunteers
once a week to write her letters
and read the mail and the bulletin
from the old church.

She has seen ninety-three springs,
and her retinas are torn.
She wants me to write
a poem about one more
so she can embrace
an invisible beauty.
She sternly forbids herself
any old-woman wandering
in April memories
of some youthful time –
like so many of her friends do.

It's dangerous, she says,
you can be lost there.

I have avoided spring poetry
this year as too trite –
the tight buds and gold-green leaves,
the saccharine litany of blooms,
like a gardening catalog
or a greeting card verse –
crocus, tulip, jonquil,
azalea, hyacinth –

the predictable verbal crumbling
of early turned soil,
old leaves and growing,
the lengthening of the light,
and always something
sentimental and not subtle
about new love.

I have no fresh words,
no vivid seeing — I am bored
with Easter metaphors and
pastel possibilities,
and I am certainly tired of love.
But for you, my old friend,
I will try.
I will welcome this season
which you will walk through,
leaning on the cane of my words
with the fierce faith
I learned from you.
I imagine all I really need to say
is here already –
spring is the time
of flowers, when something
chooses not to die.

CANA

They didn't have a phone
and so they gave a time
for the minister to call
the pay phone in the
pizza-gas station.
They arrived a day later,
clutching a license.
She was wearing pink
and he was in a white shirt,
and the buttons
stretched to expose
a triangle of T-shirt
above the belt.
They brought two friends –
witnesses, they said,
a toddler and a baby in arms.

They had put cigarettes out
in the parking lot,
and they shuffled somewhat
nervously into the church.
They had come here,
they explained,
because they discovered
those anonymous gift certificates
came from the church,
and that was the
only Christmas
the kids had last year.

She had been his brother's wife
and the children
were his brother's kids.
Both Mainers,
both from town and
didn't finish school, they
worked when they could.
And, between them,

they had about twenty teeth
which showed when they
smiled at each other.

The minister looked
at the gold rings
in her hands, engraved
with somebody else's initials.
She pulled a black robe
over blue jeans
and turned on the lights
in a sanctuary so cold
she could see her breath.
She lit a candle to exorcise
any pawn-shop bad luck,
and read the service,
blinking back
unexpected tears.

The friends witnessed,
the toddler played
under the communion table,
the baby pulled
on her mother's hair,
and the groom smoothed out
a crumpled ten dollar bill
and handed it over shyly.
The minister looked down
at the money, and entered
their names in the parish book.
It was April Fool's Day.
She decided
to ring the church bell
for them a long, long time.

COMPANIONS
"one who shares bread with"

Bates, Lee and Wilson has a decorum for it –
a long front row of seats –
family together –
then a space and a single chair
for the partner, the roommate,
the friend.
But usually I am instructed
not to say anything
about the one who buys the flowers
and cries the tears.

What kind of secret is love?

Two schoolteachers in their nineties
from Burlington,
a store clerk and a bank teller,
a public health nurse and a
history instructor –
stories of tenderness
and trust and hiding
so often hover in the over-breathed
funeral parlor air, but are
not spoken.

But this morning will be different.

Phil was born and raised in Berwick,
used to babysit his niece and nephews –
more a kid than they.
They say he taught them
to crack raw eggs on their heads.
loved to gamble – roulette,
the nightly numbers.
soft-spoken, never vindictive,
traveled to Florida, Vegas, the Islands.

owned his own shop in Kennebunk,
retired at sixty, managed
a motel for a while.
loved David for twenty-seven years,
Companions.

David was not sure if Phil was
Protestant or Catholic.
He lived a simple life,
decent, kind, full of laughter,
the golden rule.
Sometimes they went to Christmas
midnight mass.
Bates, Lee and Wilson thought –
under the circumstances –
Protestant would be safer.
I would be safer.
And as profligate as the casket spray
of sixty-four yellow roses
that counted out Phil's years
in beauty, and the
suddenly spring-warm of a day
with the smell of sea salting the air
for burying,
is the gift of my freedom

to mention – somewhere between
the gentle laughter-anecdote
about lucky numbers
and the dust and ashes prayer
where words wound to force
an ending –
God's extravagance of embrace
for men who love men and
women who love women,
and these two gentlemen who
have been for more
than a quarter of a century
sharing bread with
one another.

FISH STORY

Fishing pole for Mother's Day.
I circumnavigate it –
alien mechanism at the base,
meant for those who can
judge distance,
imagine an arc,
and relax;
bent steel barbs on string,
dangerous, I'm sure,
worms, too, (later
we will sit upon the
ground and talk about
the death of worms);
unbreakable – now
there is a challenge,
but I will rise to it
like a bobber
or belly up.

This gift – this filial
lure to Walden Pond,
this baiting of the mother,
this thin reel thing, this
angler of maternal holiday –
casts in another light
altogether the promises
of many a season.
You see, it's not the fishing
exactly that is a sinker
so to my spirits.
What is on the line here,
hooked and running
out for deep water
(poor feckless wriggling
finned creature)
is my commitment
to sit still.

Dot Joslin: a small story

The woman whose grandchildren
spoke at her funeral
had come from Birmingham, England,
to a farm in Nova Scotia,
with a note pinned to her coat,
"Dorothy Allen, age seven –
this is an orphan."

She worked on the farm long hours
all her childhood years,
and she had no friends or toys,
and she used to cry
when the sun came up
because the day would be so hard,
and she was so alone.

When she was a young woman
one of the family's daughters
brought her to Boston
where she studied practical nursing.
She needed to work very hard
for she had little education.

She nursed a young soldier,
gassed from World War I
and they fell in love.

He had come up from Maine.

Carl Joslin worked in sales,
while Dot had four children,
took in a nephew,
went to be a governess to
two generations in a wealthy
North Shore home.

Carl died when he was only fifty-six.

Dot went on living more than thirty years
for church and neighbors,
children, grandchildren.
She learned to drive at sixty-nine
and took people in nursing homes out
for rides and ice cream –
the ones who had no visitors.

The funeral went on more than an hour.
Some people said it was unseemly –
all those young men and women,
crying and telling stories
about their grandma.
Some had their own children
hugging their legs and
one carried a baby Dot had held,
in the hospital, newborn
a week ago.

The reception lasted a long time, too –
lemonade and laughter,
cookies Dot had baked
and frozen for a friend's birthday.
She had planted flowers
a few days ago for her husband,
her son and son-in-law's graves,
and her casket lay
among them.

Of course,
there were formal bouquets,
although not as many as
sometimes there are
for folks who are loved less,
and someone put a deck of cards
on the green cloth
the funeral director always uses
to mask the dirt of burying
to remember
that she played bridge,

and the littlest of great-grandchildren
gathered dandelions from
all over the cemetery
and lay them there
on her grave.
No one told them not to run.

There were very many children
and many dandelions.

SUMMER

ADAH'S SONG

The beauty burns
against the blue of morning sky
and I
in salt of weeping
look back
at the bright catastrophe
of all that meant too much
and my tears dry.

Remember me, Aunt Sarah.
Remember me,
daughters with your bellies
big with nations.
Remember me –
not as somebody's wife,
not as immobile,
but remember me
as the woman who
didn't need to run
anymore.

I have found my own place
in the wilderness.
and where I am
is holy.
I watch the sky blaze
an orange and pink and
golden past;
I lift my face to the soft rain
of falling ash;
I pray softly
and listen
to the whisper of
clean fire.

Reach out and touch me,
the smooth, the white of me;

lick the seadried taste
of my escape;
do not be afraid.
Take comfort
in me –
because
I am the woman who
stands still.

RESPIRATORY PRECAUTIONS,
ST. ELIZABETH'S HOSPITAL

The old artist lay in the white bed
in the white room,
with her tracheotomy finally taped up,
but an infection so severe
the nurse protects me from her
with plastic goggles over my eyeglasses,
mouth mask,
paper gown, latex gloves,
all secure before
I can pray with her.

I have heard Elsie's stories before –
about her honorary degree
from the art college,
her painting of greeting cards,
the mural,
cracked by time now,
in the church nursery.
Today my visit is more hurried
and I want to guide it to her health
or her faith or her future –
something vital
to an eighty-five year old woman
with a history of heart attack,
who cannot breathe or swallow,
whose husband hasn't come to see her
for a month.

But Elsie won't have it –
and I have to lean down
to hear her murmur about art and poetry,
about my poetry,
and how there is a difference between
making beauty and
doing something with it.

Then urgently, urgently,
she pulls herself up,
hunting for me in my wrapping –
words, half from her mouth,
half from the hole in her neck,
quick, light, like wind,
like the spirit of her
is speaking –

She doesn't need to tell me
I must share my words, does she?

My eyes suddenly sting
behind the shield,
and I reach out so she can hold
my hand in the hands
that painted so many colors
for so many years –
and just this one time I am glad for

respiratory precautions

to mask how ashamed I am
of my presumption
about who was going to
whisper God,
and who was going to listen.

BERAKAH

The wedding was almost stark,
eloquent in its spare
and sparing details.
The bride and groom stood alone,
silhouetted in August evening
at the edge of a garden wall
before the rabbi
who mimed the cup
of wild old covenant
with a ballet of economy,
and sang and blessed them
with a few words
that breath-sketched in Hebrew
and English polyphony
a ceremony
so simple
the bones of their love
shone through.

Later in the nighttime parking lot,
after the laughter-softness
of the party began,
and wine flowed,
the rabbi was detained
by several guests
with their unbroken glasses
who sought him out
with compliments
on the startling elegance
of his simplicity.

"I am divorcing,"
he said,
"I was singing
the least I could of pain."

YEAST

Eleanor pushes back a wisp
of grey hair,
smiles her slow smile,
and begins to talk about
her mother baking bread,
kneading her lap
as she is speaking.

She wrinkles her nose
and sniffs the air
for the baking scent
of the child she had been
running home with her brother
from school.

She cuts the edges
off the loaf
in this kitchen
of memory
and spreads sweet butter
on them,
tasting her loss.

"But Mother's been dead for twenty-five years."

It is not clear
if she is questioning
her own tears,
or trying to let them . . . rise.

LIFE STUDY

Art students gather
for life study
and pool their money
to see the lines
and curves and shadows
of a woman, and,
without ever feeling flesh,
they passionately touch
her body in paint,
or charcoal, clay, stone
hammered metal,
watercolor or pastel.

They touch the nude
curled silence of a small ear,
eyes gazing into secret space
beyond their purchase,
the small hanging breasts,
fragile boundary
of collar bone,
the pelvis hollowed slightly,
slouching buttocks
falling into thigh
without much muscle,
as leg tapers to bent knee.

The artists, with their palettes,
tools and brushes,
and umber, ocher,
violet, cerulean fingernails,
come to life study
because they expect to learn
the arrangement of ligament
and skeleton,
but instead
they dis-cover
something about truth

having no clothes,
something about holiness
that is always particular to
some imperfect anatomy,
never the ideal form
of human body,

and they begin to understand
something about
the vulnerability of art,
exposed on some wall or pedestal,
naked in a museum
or gallery
where others come to look.

VERA

She was an army nurse
and the story is told that
her tent was bombed and strafed,
in spite of the red cross
on its canvas,
once on Christmas Eve
and then a week later.
At the first attack
she made all her patients
crawl under their beds,
and she did too,
but New Year's Eve
there was one soldier
too wounded to move
and so she lay down
next to him
on the cot,
listening to enemy fire.

They gave her a medal
and featured her once
in an article about brave women
of World War II.

Now as she lies
in the shabby nursing home,
with the curling purple-flowered
wallpaper and the pink afghan
from the church ladies
on her legs,
breath rasping in and out
with long pauses between,
and the door shut
so that her last day
won't frighten others,
she remembers the warmth
of the young man's body

beside her,
and waits again
to hear
the familiar falling sound
of her death.

A Dog Story

Ed pushed a lock of white hair
out of his eyes.
He was thin
and a funny pale color
from being in the hospital
so long.
Annie had put the dog to sleep
while he was gone,
and the spider web of wrinkles
where he squinted up
to look at the sun
too many times
was damp.
"I remember another dog
we had, when we lived
in the country,
a Labrador, and
he was so afraid
of the vet
he would shake and cry
in the parking lot.

When Doc told me Blackie
was ready to die,
I carried him out
to the field back of the house
and let him lie there
for a long time,
snuffling the wind
and smelling everything
he could get his nose to—
clover-flowers, and
ground hogs
that had dug and gone,
new-wormed summer earth,
squirrel scat,
and maybe skunk

too faint for me.
When I felt the sun
deep-warm
his black old fur,
I put a thirty-eight
through the back of his skull."

JIGSAW

The old woman sits down
in front of the puzzle
in the community room at the senior center
and there are a thousand pieces
of jumbled cardboard dreams
that promise to show a mountain,
a small hut, a lake,
far from the city
outside these windows.

Every piece she turns
until it fits.
She labors long and
carefully with arthritic fingers,
making beauty
out of confusion,
so intent that we all believe
she must expect
that somehow when she finishes
she will be there

and not here.

But maybe it doesn't
have to do with geography at all –
what matters isn't the choice
between green leaf and concrete.
Maybe by this puzzling
of her hands,
she's trying to understand her life.
Finally, she remembers to start
with the borders.

Encounter with Mecholat, An Allegory

I've been to the burying place-
the cemetery where women go
with the lumpy bags
of bloody stillborn hope,
you know, the things they cannot raise,
but would kill them left inside.

Bones, too, and treasures
are for burying –
phalanges of an old love,
grip broken at the knuckle,
still seem to reach a thumb
through soil,
the jawbone of a friendship -
(we used to talk the night till dawn)
the rib of childhood,
delicate curve around the heart,
fissure-seamed from
years' gone fractures healed.

Treasures regretfully locked away in
leather-bound, brass-studded chests –
the rubies we'd worn in our hair
till someone said it was gaudy
and showed us style,
gold chains and coins
of honors earned and given,
given up,
and sparkling fantasies
of silk turbans and silver-top
slippers to twirl in ...
we tamp firm dirt over these,
when we are too wise or old or lawful
to be pirates anymore,
but mark with a cross
on the map furtively touched,
smoothed and unfolded

a hundred times,
kept safe and hidden in our pockets
for daughters.

I was leaning weary on my shovel –
I'd been burying memories,
and put some stones over them
to mark the tenderness
with something hard and worded
that other people would understand,

when I saw the woman,
bent into sunset light like
something of the earth herself –
remarked her two strange eyes,
one creased up with lines of laughter
and the other
a cup full of sorrow.

I asked what evening funeral digging
she had come to do –

"I'm burying dances..."

And I replied, "I've done that, too,
bury the ankle deep, the
dancing self kicks long
after the rhythm of life
is smothered."

"I'm burying colors..."

"Oh, they die quickly.
When you've come to the cemetery
as often as I have, you'll see that
stones and bones are white and grey,
and they, of all the hues,
are very real."

"I'm burying prayers..."

"Dig deep, dig very deep,
prayers easter-fester up,
they will not rest in peace,
and furrow-mess the smooth surface
of perpetual care.

Trust me, I've buried prayers before."

And then we were silent.
This woman with skin like
ocean floor, old bruises and
angel wings, stooped and stretched,
burying her dances,
her colors and her prayers,
until watching her bed them
in ground so full of rock,
I began to cry and knew,
as I had never known before,
in this cemetery where women go,
but do not acknowledge
each other's coming,

that only someone else
with tear streaks on dusty face
can stop interment,
and only fingers
stained green with weed
can reach out and hold and loosen
another's shovel-handle grip.
So I stopped her

and whispered,

"You cannot unearth again
this past you're graving
so lonely and deep down."

But she smiled gently at my words,
took my stiff restraining hands in hers,
and looked in my eyes where

pity wept away reserve,
and we stood four-handed
awkward in the fading light
above this place of dead
dances, dreams and hope,
this ghostly field of the
stillborn and the long-loved.

"We've come to bury
what we must bury here,
and plant what we must plant,
for we can also claim the power
of place and name

and, if you and I together say,
this is not a graveyard
any longer,
we choose to name it ... garden –
though garden means
we have to wait and tend,
not go secretly away again.
We have to stay.

But, oh, then see what will happen
to what we dare call seeds,
and, while we stand here
with dirt on our hands,

how begins the growing."

AUTUMN

ALL SOULS

In the church with the rose window
that looks like wings
to the pastor,
there are windows all around
where proud and pious Christians
of Bangor memorialize their dead
translucent.

In the church where St. Francis,
birds on his fingers, and Ruth,
gleaning golden sheaves, smile,
while a phalanx of prophets
and evangelists brood sternly down,
and St. Lucia with bread turned
to roses under her cloak
reaches out a hand,
and the newest windows are
about the beginning of time,

Matthew, the young janitor stood
and leaned against a pew
to tell me, the visitor
who came to see scripture,
about color instead –

how, in the morning, green
and yellow sparkle clear,
but later blue and purple
glow a rich brilliance, and,
then, when evening comes,
the red glass burns
so intensely
that you cannot turn
your eyes away.

When he started working here
in January,

the mornings would be so dark
he would sit a while and wait
for the colors to wake up.

He understands that stained glass
was made by artists long ago
who meant to hold on to light
so that it shouldn't die.
If I would come back later,
he would stay after hours
to unlock the heavy door
and show me the reds burning.

In the church where worshipers
have come and gone for years
with stories of their own and
bowed their heads with
some shattered
green, yellow, purple,
blue, red jagged pieces
of spirit spangled out
on wood and stone
around them and leaned
hard against the pews
with some personal heartbreak
so opaque not even noon
could light its corner,

the janitor polishes the altar table
slowly,
while the windows hold color
against the approach
of darkness.

By Clara's Grave

The father laid
strong hands
on his son's
shoulders.
A lonely wind cried
down the trees
of golden autumn,
harp-plucking the
thin branches.
One leaf,
still green, but
scarlet-edged,
blew and caught
fast in the
bronze hinges
of the long, dark
casket.
Against the rich
grain of mahogany
wood, it was
more lovely than
many flowers.
A loon rose
from the pond
into sky so
brilliant blue
it hurt the eyes.
The boy's tears fell
on the man's
hands.

THE BOY IN THE BOX AT MY FEET

is all cinder and ashes, and a smile
that could light up a room.
Carried in by the funeral director,
a young woman
in a trim black suit and high heels,
it needs to be somewhere
in the sanctuary, but not seen.
The photograph of the thirteen-year-old
should be seen.
The flowers and candles
should all be seen . . .
the bell choir from Dover,
the tall girl singing "The Rose,"
the kids who come one after another
to the microphone
to remember Andrew out loud,
and the Jews and Christians
who pray together today.

Of course, the box is packed
with tragedy –
the black calligraphy of skid
on wet pavement
thick with autumn leaves,
windscreen broken like spider webs
against utility pole.
And the box is packed
with literal remains of a kid
who loved Star Trek and Contact,
the Internet, Green Day and
the GooGoo Dolls,
of a kid who walked into the kitchen
one day and thanked his Dad
for his life.
And the box is packed
with possibilities, all burned up,
of high school and college,

of growing out the buzz cut or
shaving a not-yet-thought-of beard,
of leaving home, getting married,
having children of his own.

The funeral director asks
if she can put it under my feet,
behind the pulpit –
the boy in the box
who is all cinder and ashes,
except for the corneas and veins,
the kidneys and heart valves
that are seeing and bleeding
and peeing and beating,
and loving,
in someone else.

"Please don't stumble on him,"
she says.

No, I won't stumble on Andrew.
I look down and
he's the root growing
into the earth
of all our tears and stories.
As the rabbi says,
he's the breach in the wall
where we walk through, and
light changes to sunset
in the woods.
I will never stumble on the boy
in the box at my feet,

because the box
will never be large enough,
or deep enough, or
strong enough
to hide away the smile.

RED FLOWERS

"I can't invite my sister
because she's a junkie,"
the young man said,
speaking of his wedding,
speaking of his sister.

"She steals things."

There was a long pause
and I looked at them,
so engaged to one another,
tiptoe-foolish about matrimony
and dreams.

"There's a cactus," I said,
"I heard about long ago
from a wise old woman
who knows a lot about deserts
and thorny things,
like families and memories
and being addicted, too.
She told me that cactus
doesn't bloom
for years and years,
until one night
and one rain
changes everything."

The young woman,
in cut-offs and sandals,
suddenly looked like a bride.
She put a hand in
her young man's hand
and smiled.

"Don't worry," she said quietly,
"I will plan for rain."

KEY

The man in my prison class
held a key in his hand –
contraband I unwittingly
brought – along with
shells and stones,
an autumn leaf,
a spoon, an onion
and a dime –
things I hoped would help
the poetry begin.
He said he hadn't touched a key
for fourteen years
and his eyes glowed
and his square hands
were very gentle.
I don't know his crime –
I never ask, but I know
he won't be paroled.

He writes about sadness and prison,
a bittersweet humorous poem
about the legal brief
under his pillow that will
set him free.
He wouldn't read the poem
he wrote about the key,
but he read one about
sitting close to his mother
watching television
when she had a rare day off
and he was a child
in the projects –
and the perfume of her,
and the feel of her clothes,
and safety.

INTER-FEAR

Wife and daughter were shot
in the head, sleeping.
Two days later
the man was killed
by the police in Nebraska.
The girl, who was the
same age as my daughter,
performed Indian dances at school.
The newspaper shows
her beautiful young face
above the flowing
yellow silk of sari.

I recognized the apartment building –
our address in Brookline,
when I brought my baby home
from Beth Israel Hospital.
I remember the park
across the street,
perfect for stroller and sheltie.
I remember the Italian family
who ran the fruit stand,
the Chinese couple
who had the convenience store,
the college students
with their Friday night parties,
and spice-smells of cooking
from around the world.

And I remember that on
weekday afternoons,
when most people were working,
I would listen to blows and cries
from the apartment
near the elevator doors,

and I would creep down the corridor
with my newborn in my arms
to ask if she was OK.

She would open a few inches,
peering with her bruised eyes,
and say, "please go away",
and I would return
to my maternity leave,
and pour a large glass
of red wine,
and turn up the TV loud
at four o'clock for the
Streets of San Francisco.

Of course, this is a different woman.
We moved away long ago.

CONVERSATION WITH KAREN

Yellow leaves are falling outside the window
and the air is absolutely still –
straight down they fall,
and the woman in the wheelchair
with a purple birthmark on her face
and a smile like she has a secret,
and eyes set wide and open,
disconcerting,
as if life amazes her,
and the soft furriness of hair
just beginning to grow back
has pushed away from the stove
with her cup of tea.

She is planning it after Christmas,
after she makes gingerbread houses,
gives gifts, sings carols,
after she is able to break
through her father's defenses,
and he agrees to carve
a wooden bench to mark her grave,
so people can go there
to rest their hearts for a while,
and after she is sure her sons
and her husband will not be afraid
of the awkward good-byes
or angry at her body or the pain.

The October afternoon sky
glows early vesper-grey
with the iridescence of autumn rain
that has not yet begun
though the air is full and unshed with it.
The birch leaves, yellow against
white bark and black soil,
continue to fall –
single, gentle and heavy,

inevitable as old psalms,
detaching from the branches
in windless descent.

She needs about ten more weeks.

RESURRECTION

We remember and celebrate the life
of Bill Micchelli –
the words come softly –
how he laughed, always laughed,
and stray dogs and cats came to him
and children loved him.

We remember and celebrate the life
of Bill Micchelli –
born in New Jersey,
loved to cook Italian food,
has a daughter somewhere
in California,
prayed every night to St. Jude,
was writing the book of
all his stories.

We remember and celebrate the life
of Bill Micchelli –
worked in drug rehab
and halfway houses,
listened to teenaged men
till they knew their telling
mattered to him,
and they opened the
fists of young anger
to reach for life.

We remember and celebrate the life
of Bill Micchelli –
loved Barbara for nine years
of touching
and not touching,
planned to cheat death
and be married next month.

We remember the death of Bill Micchelli

but we do not celebrate death –
not the dark whisper of AIDS
that breathes time into the heart,
not the loss of the laugher,
the lover of strays,
the man who could have
pulled more needles
out of young boy's arms.

And still so softly the words of
remembering were said
in the too-smooth
funeral home rooms,
where every day is a new death
and old hymns like stale smoke,
hover in the air.

Then into the room came the ·
thin black boy in the black jacket,
black pegged pants,
silver belt,
chains on his ankles,
and two policemen,
with carefully empty faces,
accompanying him
for the five minutes
the law gives to grief.

He shuffled to the basket
of photographs
set on the cool marble table
for friends to choose,
took one that showed
the profile of a black-haired man
with a pony tail and an earring,

The boy gave Barbara a kiss,
and stood looking
at the flowers,
until the policemen

led him away.

And the words of the service
began softly – ever
so softly – again,
as funeral words do,
not meaning much, but
shaping the silence,
while the heart folds over
the intimate and puts the
name away.

We remember and celebrate
the resurrection of
Bill Micchelli –
he is no longer dead,

look out the door –
he just changed another life.

AFTER THE FALLING LEAVES—EPILOGUE

AT THE GALLERY

During his blue period,
when he was very young,
Picasso sought
permission to paint
the patients
of the Saint-Lazare Hospital
for incurable illnesses.

The painting in the corner –

passed quickly by the surge
of Museum patrons
who maneuver their
slow dance, not touching
elbows or eyes,
isolated by the headphones
which guide them from
selected picture
to selected picture and
tell them what
to see and feel –

is of a prostitute
with venereal disease.

She wears the white cap
with which such women
are identified.
Her clothes are blue,
the background is blue,
and her face is blue.
Her legs are stretched out
awkwardly in front of her,
and she is cradling
an infant in her arms.
She gazes down on him
and the child looks back,

icon, implacable.

Nobody is looking
at this painting,
too much God and madonna,
and it's not
part of the recorded tour.

FOR FLORENCE DUDLEY

She lay in the white
                    bed,
frail, tiny, eyes
            barely open,
One hundred and two
years old next week,
bones fragile as moth's wing,
and said so clearly,
in the midst of
            something
                    else ...

"Life is short."

"Why Florence," said I,
"How can you say that
when you've had the longest
                    life
I've ever known?"

"Oh, my dear," said
            the old woman,
"it goes so quickly by,
            and I
have not had
                    time
for half the things
I want to do."

ABOUT THE AUTHOR

Maren C. Tirabassi is a poet, liturgical writer, and pastor of the Northwood Congregational Church, U.C.C., in Northwood, New Hampshire. She teaches the writing of poetry in churches, schools, and prisons and is a frequent conference and seminar leader. An Iowan, Tirabassi holds degrees from Carleton College, Union Theological Seminary (NY), and Harvard Divinity School, and has served six New Hampshire and Massachusetts churches over the last twenty years. Her books are *Touch Holiness* (Pilgrim Press, 1990, with Ruth C. Duck), *Gifts of Many Cultures: Worship Resources for the Global Community* (United Church Press, 1995, with Kathy Wonson Eddy), *An Improbable Gift of Blessing* (United Church Press, 1998, with Joan Jordan Grant), and forthcoming from United Church Press – *Blessing New Voices: Prayers of Young People and Worship Resources for Youth Ministry*. She is collaborating with Charles McCollough on *Faith Made Visible: Shaping the Human Spirit in Sculpture and Word*. Maren frequently performs her work and tours with poet Diana Durham and short story author Rebecca Rule in "What Lies Beyond – A Journey for Three Voices," a performance funded in part by the New Hampshire State Council on the Arts and the National Endowment for the Arts, which premiered in Portsmouth, New Hampshire, at the McDonough Street Studio in 1998.

The author welcomes inquiries about her books, workshops, and performances by mail to:

271 Lafayette Road, Portsmouth, NH 03801-5433